Marginal Verse

poems by

Jamie Silvonek

Marginal Verse

Cover design by Catherine Weiss

Edited by Ally Ang and Josh Savory

www.gameoverbooks.com

to my mom

Part One

Part One

Where I End, Prison Begins

So long since I've been touched
my nerve endings mistake fabric for flesh.
Senses dulled, I confuse my feet for concrete
and I live by plangent bells here. They ring
at set times but they never stop sounding for me.
A shrill playlist screams like the youth
I robbed myself of. Reversed,
I don't bleed anymore.
I feel a wet warmth on my lips,
finger my nostrils' menstruation.
Now, it's my shirts that are stained.
Clocks anchor and hypnotize as I stare at the hands
cycling through the hours
while my own wither.
Prison begins behind closed eyelids:
stirring from visions, noticing my freshly mutilated skin;
faces, names, lifetimes in the cell with me
but I'm alone still.
I sleep obliviously.
When I wake, I realize
I was watching someone else folded in their dark cell
as I held my breath—

I know that when I end, prison will begin.

Death by Incarceration

decades pass by I tick off with my fingers
and now that my palm is about to be open
my eyes will close for the last time
the world enclosing me
this industrial bubble of concrete and steel
has seen little change over these years
but from what I've heard
I would find the society that lies outside of it
to be unrecognizable
as time shuffles by
the hope I once had has seeped from me
and I no longer wish to know what lies beyond
this barbed wire and gated sky
now, all that I am is old and tired
and what I desire more than anything
is to rest
and close my eyes this final time

Erasure

I am Hatshepsut
whatever I accomplish in this fleeting life
men in robes will obscure
I am Paul
I scrawl these last words from a prison
hoping one day they will be read
and understood
I am Cassandra
I couldn't bear the price he offered me
now no one will believe my truth
and I am condemned to roam this abyss
screaming my story into its vastness
hearing clips of my cries echoed back to me
the darkness enfolds me and I welcome it
the only sure thing I've ever known
the void within me cracks open to converge with nothing
where everything can begin.
I am home.

Identity Politics

I had written a chapbook's worth of poems
about being a woman in prison.
I trashed it
because the publishers didn't want to be reminded
of their privilege
and that female convicts touch themselves at night.

Some liberalgradkid
thought I was tragic and intellectual.
I told him I'm bad news
and a good day is one where I've found the motivation to shower.

A bitch freebleeding while cuffed and shackled:
illicit, triple x,
unapologetic.

After Etheridge Knight's "As You Leave Me"

It is now time and has always been.
You assume I don't but a woman always knows,
knows a man's muscular hardenings / his (animal) thoughts.

Cast as an object of Desire
records will spin and soothe, get glitched on repeat.
I've evolved to fit
the stretch marks and dimples that confound you;
no metamorphosis has kissed your sad bones.

What do you know of full cells and empty streets?
Of their converse?
A Woman is reborn every time
she chooses to walk away,
and a man dies.

I Was Only Following Orders

I thought the boys would understand
but their death machines weren't made for my hands
triggers weren't shaped for frail fingers
and they've never tasted the soot and shit that I have

how did it feel to take innocent lives?
I asked the haunted man with dead eyes
even though he was charged with my custody
I knew he was like me, he too was hollow inside

we blew up a bus in afghanistan, he said
there were over 30 women and children
it haunts me to this day
I cannot unsee the things I've seen

I don't believe in patriotism and I don't know war, I said
but I know guilt, I know it well
do you believe in mercy?

he looked at me with his expressionless eyes
it depends.
the law is the law.
if we condoned murder, there would be anarchy.

Positive Affirmations

I slept haunted by my failure and awoke to the mission of a new day in which I will not cut I will not binge I will not purge I will not starve myself I will not exercise for hours and hours until I pass out I will not sleep all day or deprive myself of sleep I will not stare at myself in the mirror and loathe what I see I will not be disgusted by my facial deformity I will love myself I will be healthy I will not grab handfuls of my fat and spiral I will forgive myself for what I did I will look forward I will not devise suicide plans as a coping skill because I am a coward and I cannot follow through I have quit every project I have ever endeavored upon I didn't have the courage to stop him so where could I find the courage to stop my own weak heart nowhere I was never disciplined enough for ballet or piano or soccer or field hockey or lacrosse or french horn and now even pathetic prison attempts at writing at guitar at painting at college at self-destruction at activism who would want to read my clumsy words hear my lisping voice I know nothing nothing except the gulag I've been caged in since just after my 14th birthday and the childhood cages that primed me for this confinement this stasis this morbid cycle of punishment in which I torture myself more than they ever could I mutilate my body to prove I am still sovereign over my own flesh I inculcate my mind with its worthlessness so that my network cannot be hacked by the hegemony their malware programming me telling me nothing I do will ever be enough I will never get better I am structurally incapable of goodness I am criminal I am deviant I am disposable I am other I am hopeless how do I face today this day with the glare of the suicidal sun accusing me like the police did it's better to lie here in my safe sweat-rancid cocoon this dark coffin rank of my rotting corpse it's easier to hide under these womblike sheets waiting for the sun to commit its seppuku to be born again at dawn waiting to die again tonight so I can try anew tomorrow

Justice

My hair like my cares

       thinning

              falling

sewn into my head,
golden crops at harvest
departing as taxis.

No,
none of this has been fair
but the cabbies still whistle
as the farmer runs his comb through my wheat.

First Person Limited

Trapped is this mediocre body, this singular view
possessed by these insane narrators that never cease
shackled to the perpetuity of breath.
Neurotic, neurotic
psychotic most likely.
You're probably not, although I am.
A fly trapped inside this skull,
inside this hermetically sealed cage.
Wherever it is that I am
and this fate that I've been sentenced to.
Well, I did knock, but nobody answered:
the door cracked open
and all I heard was my voice echoed back to me by the void.

Y.O.U. (Youthful Offender Unit)

we're playing rap music
from one of the stations on the flat screen
that the state bought us and doesn't think we deserve
as we sit here in the waning light of the afternoon
playing cards and braiding each other's hair
with grease-slicked fingers and comebacks on our lips
this ancient room rank with hormonal sweat and mold
has become an artifact of our commonwealth's
colorful history
just as we have
our mindstates are youthful and ready
like our poised adolescent bodies
and even though in our present state we have little to do
nowhere to go
and not much to show for the nothings we've accomplished
I know in this frenzied salmon moment of laughter and r&b
and good natured insults
that I'm down,
I'm down for anything

Statement Piece

If you have more to say
put this upside down cross necklace on,
it makes for good publicity.

As your role model said,
seize the moment and let the consequences be damned,
spit out the nails rusting in your mouth.

One act of revolution can affect generations.
Marching in the streets is not nearly enough;
whooping alone has yet to get anyone what they need.

Sit alone in the stillness of a quiet dark room
and think of the most provocative, shocking thing
the masses have never seen.
This is not a poem one can finish:
it's a warm-up.

Childless Cat Lady Accepts Aloneness

Weight gain, socks damp with sweat, crinkly eyes
arriving decades early and unsolicited.
All you want is a good fuck,
the kind that will make your insides puddle syncopated
onto the floor and numb you in the way you need.
You didn't dream of living and dying alone
but now you understand it's the way things must be.
Love has become sticky honey, messy paint
a cloying perfume you once adored
that now suffocates.

Bulimia Nervosa

never was silence as dense as this
skin freckled pink by exploded capillaries
cosmic petechiae betray the suffocating space
where fingers escape

cavity mottled nebulae
event horizon of expulsion
the radius of my bloated body expands
with every swallowed star and acid stain

no newness here: only dangling uvulae
sway, the entropic pendulums timing self-decay
in this void no tardigrades can survive
shy moons wane their slow deaths
while I gum my familiar porcelain retrograde

You Ask Me What I Fear

and I falter.
There is so much to fear that it is futile to be afraid.
It makes much more sense to greet life with acceptance,
to bravely face the inevitable unknowns
that accompany the brevity of sentience.
What I do know is how much I fear
your chicory lips not pressed against mine
in this most singular moment.

Memento Mori

Buzzing in the skull, in the skull.
Memento mori,
the clogged sink.
Pump the hole with
your wrinkling hand. Smell the drain,
the excrescence of your mouthwaste
& the sludge your guilty palm shed.
Complicit fingers, say no more. Don't speak
your tacit indictment. Just pick the particles
from the bowl your head could fit in.

Small Talk

Slogging my boots through drenched
leaves pasted onto the cement
making autumn music.
You ask if we can talk about something else.
The tree glows yellow illuminated by the streetlamp
while I shiver at the length of your eyelashes.
Winter is nipping at our ears
but somehow death seems so distant.
I ask what you believe in.
You say I don't know, I don't know.

Silver

frost on the pane of the window
that gives me a glimpse of freedom
silver
the wash of the moon casting the world
in a silken shadow
silver
the scars self-slashed on the arms of those suffering
wrangling demons of guilt that can only be bled out
bronze when inflicted
silver when healed
these marks of hideous tragedy
on beautiful bodies

Strange Goddess

Dead moths hang from your ceiling
suspended by guitar strings.
Yoked to this room by an orchestral sound
or maybe it was a woman wailing.
No light can enter here;
there are no fissures the photons can penetrate.
The darkness here is whole, it is complete,
unlike so many things.
Unlike me.
What brought these moths here,
dusted flutterings wavering drunkenly
towards brightness?
Strange goddess,
I can't tell if you're the light the moths sought
or the darkness they died in.
No forms chisel against the obsidian
except my own languid thoughts;
I can no longer hear the women calling my name,
I can no longer hear the fanfare
from the depths of this cave.
Strange goddess,
soon I too will hang from twine,
a marionette in repose suspended in time—

Insomnia

tell me what it means, what it means
I've been sitting on this floor all night long
the radiator hissed
& told me what you did
its rusted warmth chilled me
I grew heavy
& the concrete cracked beneath my weight
a great horned owl came to the window
& told me the dawn was coming soon
but the filth of this small room
has not yet been bathed in light

Intergenerational Trauma

Something old,
something new,
something buried in these woods.
You know, out back decomposing in the fecund earth.
What is it? A human skull?
No, nothing that grotesque.
Maybe it is our dreams,
abandoned and buried:
buried, right at the murder scene
for our progeny to discuss and mourn
and write shitty verse about.

Workplace Relations

drink this water and die
there is no hemlock here, I won't toast to my treason
black mold corrodes the pipes I imbibe from
so I inspect my mouth daily in the distorted mirrors
moss grows on my uvula & I know small purple mushrooms
line my esophagus
the backs of my teeth are painted brown
tilt my head back so you can see
I'll display my throat in total submission
a beta wolf conceding
map my jugular as we drink chablis
plan my destruction while we pretend
this cloudy water is white wine
suicide by cop applies to any man in uniform
I'm little red riding hood cloaked in brown
this enchanted forest is guarded by sentinels & razor wire
your disguise lured me in
& it's a shame I'll never know what face it hides
would you find me as intriguing
if I wasn't the mysterious caged thing
that you are tasked with feeding from your hands
but the animal outside this tame forest
that stalks right past you

What I Think About When I Think About Existence

In my insignificance
I yearn to be swallowed
by something greater than myself.
The blood-blistered whites of my eyes flit
as I search the sweeping blue
for more than this
wretched reality;
this doleful promise
of inevitable human suffering
and the same funereal days
the same fulvous sun
that will rise continuously until it burns out
or my own nova is smothered first.

Dead Weight

how much does a body weigh?
a body
like mine
with life pulsing through it still
for some time
how much does a body weigh?
the same body
but mine
freshly devoid of life
cooling, stiffening every second
pants soaked with piss
and glassy eyes clear of the guilt
it will no long feel
for learning the heaviness
when another life hangs
on this wretched body of mine

Don't Count Down the Years, It Will Drive You Crazy

Brevity clotted.
If you can't unite, disperse
as permanence tends to.
Eke out your hours:
days won't offer you
the promises they used to.

Results Found for "Humane Animal Trap"

there's a creature inside of me
trying to claw her way out
I feel her at the roof of my mouth
making me screamshout
for Mercy
maybe she's the reason
I'm in a cage
why I'm in chains
why I'm slowly dying here alone

this is what a wounded animal looks like
I'm sorry this isn't more exciting

How to Be Beautiful in Prison: A Tutorial

chalk dusted on her eyelids like a butterfly
pencil lines her brows
the thinnest twigs of a winter tree
grease and pen ink coat her lashes
parted so meticulously
with the frayed strands of a used toothbrush
what eyes does she impress
when everything is brown in her world
every being cloaked in sepia tones of monochromaticity
she tries to defy the spectrum
with contraband disguises
but her avian display is missed
by colorblind eyes evolved to detect only
the threatening rustle of movement
the subtle gradients of shadow
masks not painted but scraped
out of the dirt and grime in the crevices of her hole
her cave-like cage
cracks encrusted with filth the only penetrable fissure
which the sound of her chest heaving can escape through
unmuffled, but soiled
hertz of sound strain against shades of brown fabric
hushed by polyester cotton blend
the chemical dye that bleeds every white a shamed pink
muted colors amplified by each watercolor tear
every pastel saturated by the shuddering, expectant anxiety
in the moment before being noticed
and forgotten by eyes that slide
to other umbers
the hues between seen and unseen, recognized and invisible
are only variants of the well-worn brown
she tears and paints and stitches illicitly
to maybe find another bird as rare as she
a winged thing whose eyes have mutated to see
her desperate screams of colored difference

Whistleblowing with Lips Sewn Shut

systematized gravitas
stringy hair and coffers tossed into a cluttered desk

old papers that will never have
steely eyes roving them again

and only a smattering of practical knowledge
in this whole damned place

a life lived in surfeit
but the tragedies are only now learning blade tricks

the bards of this crowd see through canines
the government stole their eyes for exposing truths
in terse verse

I don't have a conscience
only code telling me what to do

Creation Myth

the tip of my e-cig glows red like a cellphone tower
when I inhale / exhale
gossamer webs of ecstasy in my solitude
the barred window is cracked open like my skull
my brain seeps out onto the bed
its juices drip from the bunk and piddle to the floor
neurons float around the room like fireflies
and my electricity lights the space
a shrine to my new power
through the window night sounds call to me
the darkness is so inviting
I know she will envelop me
impregnate me with mystery
and I will create in that fertilizing night
howling as I birth those words
the day has feared since he began
I was banished from paradise
and I will cast myself out of hell:
I crawl through the bars and
fall to the ground
so I can begin

String Theory

tell me when you can't see my hands anymore
I am extending them
just beyond your vision

the strings of this fabric
one so fine and final
I know each thread contains
a universe of particles
all more interconnected
than I could ever conceive
than I could ever be
within the confines of
my own small world

humming, buzzing
the divine sounds
that spheres make
as they collide
or are they strings
bisecting the instrument
harmonizing to my demise

Beat: Eating Cement

numb concrete saws the soles of
my feet flinching and callous against
the grit which blurs into a
smooth nothing a
disorder that decays and
disassembles before I can find
favor in its finality

Cold or Not

Stone by stone, Jung built himself the tower that
reflected his soul, added rooms and floors
as his consciousness expanded
and his understanding grew.
I've never had the patience to create anything by hand,
never had the grit to see any task through.

Jung carried each stone from the quarry
knowing the greatness he could coax from it,
bearing the weight of a hundred others.
I am unbalanced, a misplaced stone.
I would collapse in the dust of the quarry
and stare at the craggy walls knowing
I could never make anything more beautiful
than their silence.
My hands grasp for tools I'll never learn to use.

Jung carved into his tower
that God is present, cold or not,
but I've never felt God in any temperature.
I didn't feel God on a nameless winter night as I
shuddered against a prison cell's broken radiator
bundled in damp layers and starved for warmth,
when the fluorescent lights illuminated the snow like
a cell phone screen, voided the stars and cast shadows of
the barbed wire into my cage like
shadows of tinsel.

God, thaw my heart, carve something beautiful
from my hideousness.
I am the archetype of bloodied underwear and
evanescent accomplishments.

Abolition

encrypted data, trolls, the bloodstains on my underwear
you know, whimsical things:
the microcosms of much larger machines
evidence left behind by capitalists at the crime scene

some people take apart electronics and become overwhelmed
so they acquiesce and buy replacements
others can rebuild the objects, and do
but on occasion like to dismantle
for the sake of dismantling
leave deconstructed things in stripped states
for the sake of abolition

Carceral Eugenics

lock up any nubile woman for a quarter of a century
and see if her ovaries are still functioning
any evil woman, any seductress
too loud, too opinionated, too revolutionary
or possessing too much of any particular quality
has each set of her lips sewn shut
in a legally prescribed and physically painless way
I too would like to raise a human
see my love reflected in their milky eyes
hear their nonsensical gurglings
I too have pounded tables
spat and shrieked to get what I desired
I suppose that even though I am sovereign over my own body
the state has determined me to be
undeserving
of ever being a mother naturally
and no child is safe
being raised by a criminal who didn't birth them, apparently
sad:
all too often
those who have inflicted the most pain
are the ones who have learned
to nurture life's fragility

Hysteria

my organs are coveted as if lined with copper
grifters with masks and latex glove
scramble to unravel my coils
how much does a uterus go for on the black market?
they called me a Criminal and I am the sum of my parts
but they pretend my innards are blameless
somehow untainted by my badness
my sex membranes are ripe and functioning
they ooze and throb and respond to my index finger
my clock ticks until the one thing I can offer
is harvested from me
capitalism has forced women to choose between
their own career or their own family
the eggs of women perched behind oak desks shrivel
while mine wait to be fertilized
bleeding out into prison-issue tampons
that shed their bleached cotton inside me
women here barren without cause or justification
hysterectomies as prevention, not a last resort
they don't fear us reproducing, making more bodies
they can cage and profit from
is there a scientific need to research female sex organs?
are the infertile elite buying the wombs of the disposable?
no, I'm just being hysterical
my uterus rising from my deep to float around my body
a jellyfish inducing paranoid delusions
my hysteria is strictly female
feral in its hormonal irrationality
I will put my feel in the rusted stirrups
breathe in their dreamtime gasses
let them cure me of this insanity

Cheryl Louise

I hope you know everything I do is for you.
All my life you urged me to shine for myself
but after what I've done
the idea of a self doesn't appeal much anymore.
I want to be the woman you were in life
but it seems like I can't even come close.
You were soft around the edges where I'm hard and jagged
patient and kind where I've been worn ragged.
How can I move on from this
when I still see you everywhere
in everything?
It may be your blood in my veins
but that doesn't make us the same.

Self-Sabotage as Performance Art

Amateur poet and professional liar,
verses seen but never read.
Not paid for my lurching words
but please tender my pain,
always nodding off during lectures.
Self-stuck in this cycle of touching the stove
I've touched a thousand times before and
have never felt.
Pain tries to teach us.
Most students get it
the first or second time;
others fail,
doomed to repeat the same course
for the rest of their lives.
A half-woman stares at herself for hours in the mirror each day
because she can't bear what she sees;
maybe if someone else can
she will be able to.
Love for some is the sound of
a shattering fragile thing
the despair in knowing you've really done it this time, kid
and the hopeless thrill in trying to salvage the wreckage anyway
because the infinitesimal chance of redemption
is worth every foolish sacrifice.
Shrieks and slammed doors and jealousies like jewels of fire,
how you only believe someone loved you after you've annihilated them
when they've retired from your tests and games, your dualities
and you're left with your half-face, your half-life
thinking maybe this is why you're alone again
but are jolted by the memory that
you forgot to turn the stove off before you left.

Psychiatric Observation

voices slide and slither like snakes
the walls screech
fighting for your rapt attention
you can't remember how long you've been in this warped room
with its vanilla walls and perpetual light
the barred sky that sings to you sweetly at night
it seemed one moment you were walking the yard
and now you are forgotten
diurnal events of dank food and even more dank
the cyan jumpsuit you haven't changed
the feral odor your body has taken
you're numb
at least you have what little property The Man allows
maybe you'll feel something again
if you lather your dry, reeking body in petroleum jelly
and light up a cigarette
give that snickering lighter a flick or two

How to Affect Change, for Beginners

There's nothing you can say that will dissuade me.
I'm going to do it
I'm going to
I'm going to leave this indelible mark on history
ensure no one ever forgets the sound
of these shots ringing out.
When they don't listen, you make them.
Shove the barrels of their guns down their throats
until they see your humanity too.
A time comes when the teachings of the great masters
are no longer pertinent
and you have no choice
but to undo your lotus pose
and shake out your tingling legs.
We can be better than this violence, they plead
but I never claimed to be anything other than human.

It looks like it's just you, me, and the taxi driver.

Part Two

Anthropocene Love

no shortage of red meat in the abattoir of our affair
these corpses didn't emit bovine methane in their lifetimes

we can't scream at each other over hamburgers and milkshakes
but we can bicker eating this fatty meat with fries
passive aggression and deathly silence
like the frozen torsos stored in the freezer

I'll roleplay the butcher chopping up limbs
and you can be the carnivorous patron
cadaverous face betrayed
because you expected venison
not the other woman splayed
on the table, thighs bloody
and yawning on the slab

ask the price of her head and I'll counter
with the cost of antipathy, collateral damage
a death toll to balk at

this climbing climate leaving humans
the only sustainable crop
dooms people like us to the fate
of either the weakest mouse pup
or its mother exacting a late-term abortion

no lucky love in Darwin's game
of survival
when you're triangulated an upside down and
arcane pink
when the complex profits off your
caged body
your contained and controlled movements
powering their prophesied machine

Honeymoon Phase

In the backseat of your Camaro
everything was not final,
it was only just beginning.
Our collective breath fogging up the glass
concealing us like a secret steaming spring
hidden high in the Himalayas;
running up and down the snowy streets of a small, quiet town
chasing each other like children
peals of raucous laughter trailing behind us.
We were clad in combat boots and leather jackets
(mine white, yours black)
because the world was something yet to be conquered by us.

If I could have foreseen what would ensue
would I still have blushingly accepted your first kiss
on our second date
after spurning all of your other advances?
On our third,
would I still have realized
that I could deny you nothing?

Before Your Absence Became Safety, I Used to Miss You

This shirt that you left with me
smells of you still:
musky and earthen
sweat and sandalwood
cigarette smoke
leaves me aching.
It is gray,
a split triangle stamped on the back
and the name of the institution you whoop for
emblazoned across the front.
Don't go anywhere,
GO anything:
this thin fabric is not solace enough.
We made a trade:
you have my silk scarf,
fuchsia like the flush of my cheeks
heady with the scent of vanilla
on my sanguine skin.
You tell me you sleep with my scarf every night,
clutch it while listening to me purr over the phone.
I'm glad to know you're not the only one—
the way I cling to your shirt at night,
contrasting my soft naked body
with rough blended cloth.

All of My Vices Are Killing Me

You're a bad habit I've taken up,
a tabagie.
We meet daily
sucking smoke into brushfire dry lungs
thick with singeing suffering.
Gaze hazier than your cigarette smog,
your vulpine smirk stained yellow
from coffee beans and nicotine.
More addicted to you than I am to caffeine,
nursing you like a cuppa
in a very public café.
Lust a thick tar that coats, smothers, suffocates—
here, let me crack a window so these fumes can ventilate.

If You Be Johnny Depp, I'll Be Amber Heard

Sadness inspires me
and I am pathetic for it.
I am counting on you to disappoint
in some melodramatic way
and I'll write a maudlin poem
about how I miss snubbing you.
I don't exactly relish being a degenerate;
it's your imagined hands wringing my neck I savor
as you concede that I'm the best.
My life, marked by bathos and inertia.
You sound so contrite
when you haven't answered
my collect calls in a while.
It's been so long since I've had a good time
                    that I'm not even interested anymore.

Dear/Deer

I'll kiss my own wounds
just to prove
that I don't need you to do it.
I'll cause my own injuries
just to see how you react,
with urgency or indifference
to my blatant cries for attention.
You never really gave a fuck about me, did you?
I'll answer my own question
as the spots on my back fade,
as velvet button horns push through my skull.
Fawns hide in the undergrowth for a while,
then they resurface on spindly legs
and maybe get shot
by a hunter just as apathetic as you are.

Gaslight Broken

Your shadow on the ground
casts distorted images before me
flickering in the changing light
vacillating like we so often do.
I will wait, hoping for something tangible
or for some brief glimpse of you.
Instead I am met with a cave's allegory
and I am the dazed prisoner chained to the wall
watching your form flicker before my straining eyes.
I'm not sure where to go from here;
maybe I should break my chains
and extinguish your light source
so you can't continue to elude me.

Daddy Can't Fix This

It was for you I clipped my tongue
bled crimson into a porcelain sink
red on white, a familiar scene.
It is with these words I speak my truth
but not for me;
these words are meant for you.
In Italy when you visited the Trevi
you cast every single wish upon me.
You still think of me across an ocean:
you toss coins to my days,
you see my face in the art.
I would walk with you amidst the sprawling crowds,
find a piece of home in a land so far away.
The truth is, none of this can ever happen
because I spilled the blood that bore my blood into the sink
before I clipped my tongue
and even though it is what we both want the most
things will never be the same again.

You Made Me

You're the murderer in this florid lucid dream
my tongue like a dog's
panting to lick the vinegar salt from your feet.
I throb with want for the first time
since I watched a movie about torture
when I was six years old.
Craven, sick
demented, sadistic—
I know I am all of these things.
Muffled screams from the closet
are only your conscience calling you home.
If you steady your breath
we can pretend this moment doesn't exist
that we aren't the unmasked monsters
our parents used to warn us about.
Come, crawl into this shared space
into this fatuous darkness.
Understand if only for a heartbeat
this is the same blood that gave us life.

What Is Done to Us, We Repeat

Newly christened, freed
some other blushing iris will follow me.

Our tryst was lightning split open,
bent into something bright and hideous.
I knew that we tended towards entropy
like our universe,
like this gulping concrete,
chaos inside of chaos.

To you I was a VR headset providing rich stimuli
on your brief hiatus from real life;
to me you were reality, even though I didn't understand why
you screamed at me when I tried to touch you.

The crude robot that gets left to a soggy cardboard box
in the amateur inventor's garage
when their tinkering produces a more novel machine.

A Case for Suicide

Drag my water-rotted, bloated body from the river
and if the creatures haven't yet devoured my eyes
you might understand why I did it.
My heart trilled in my chest and my lungs screamed for air
but these instincts were overridden;
when the desire for death is too strong
nature is rendered impotent against it.
If you were in my head at the time,
you would understand why I did it;
the guilt gnawing through to my bones
like the fish in the depths.

It really isn't hard when you put your mind to it.
After all,
if you really did kill once,
it should be easy to kill again.

Body of Memory

always one limb of my body
bouncing, twitching rapidly
a small dog
riddled with anxiety
trembling
with every short breath I take
flinching
at every male movement
remembering
grabbinghandspryingopenforcinggently
shattering
a belief / a hope / an image
I never knew I held
until it splintered inside me
and I bled out the detritus

Too Much

My whole life
I've worried about not being enough.
I was always too much,
or at least that was the complaint.
I bubbled over.
No one could contain me in my vastness
especially not you.
Me: imponderable, didactic
sick of this stalemate that will not secede
until my swollen tongue protrudes from bruised lips.
You, tortured by the lives led by others
while you expound your unscientific beliefs
and curse the star that reminds you of me.

I Can Be That

This crooked smile, this contorted cheek—
betrayal has never felt so sweet.
An act of treason committed by one you thought you knew
fuels the kind of rage
that curls toes in ecstasy
digs pointed teeth into slicked hide.
If this is what it comes down to—
scrubbing prayer white shoes for hours—
vicariously scouring your umber gaze off my skin
then disregard me.
I'll wear dirty shoes
be the filthy whore
you told me I was
because I'm selfish
and I never know when to stop.

Revenge Fantasy

I'll smear your blood,
bedaub the walls of the house you wish you grew up in.
It's the only thing I seem to think about anymore,
the sole subject I can write about.
I know it would be an orgasmic release—
a sneeze, a shiver
a fire on a bitter night—
to watch your hewn face plum as I strangle you.
Instead I become nonaction, smoldering
as you forget everything I wish I could beat into your head.
Too vain to break my knuckles punching closed doors
I'll tamper open other locked gates
and maybe one will lead to something.

Talking About Feelings

All I am is anger
smoldering beneath my skin.
The adrenaline rage is all I can feel
in its dizzying ecstasy
until it fuses into
the hurt that birthed it.

It's like the hurt muddled everything—
I can't tell what I'm feeling anymore.
How do I know
if the effervescence in my stomach
is anxiety or excitement?
Is it guilt or gratitude
that swells my throat shut?
Are my cheeks flushed red
out of shame, or a crush?

I am an ancient hominid stargazing
through the Kepler telescope
of my own emotions.
I can't begin to comprehend
what the pinpricks of light mean.
How do I know what they represent--
where one ends and another begins?
They are heaven and hell
and the gods themselves war
in the blackness above
and within the body
filled with the darkness below.

The Difference

Sickly breath hovering in this moment
muffled, so as to not offend.
Death has its own scent, murder its own rankness.
Don't ask me how I know the difference.
I tried to avoid wearing white for this occasion,
but some realities are unavoidable.
Don't look at my shoes
white leather stained brown with coffee.
Sinuses clogged, I steal a breath through any other opening.
What fate does the collapse of my chest belie?
Will the coroner be able to guess the cause
as I crouch here under your coffee table
in your fetid living room
heaving every eroded yellow tooth from my own mouth
now gaping, now drooling
while you pleasure yourself in the pooling blood
wearing your same puckish smile:
all white.

Arachnophobia

Atypical in my turpitude, callow in my amusements,
      I shrink myself into a shadow and vanish,
            throwing glamor.

The hovering spider laughs at my witticisms,
      I see you through its many eyes.

You cannot tell who or what I am,
      I have every disguise at my command.

I'm every nameless passing stranger
      in the constriction of your nervous throat.

I crawl through your room at night on eight spindly legs
         just for fun.

Kill me and I multiply
      my atoms can accommodate any rearrangement.

Not an insect or a contortionist but a great listener,
      the camouflage your carpet provides
         means I can do this all day.

Rorschach Test

The inverse of infinity
is the inside of your eyelids.

I've been thinking about dismembering you,
but I'm not sure what I would do with the gallons of blood.

Don't worry, don't worry: you aren't missed.
I've been having fun by myself
drawing images of primitive snowmen
and listening to Eminem.

Someone told me once that a person's best company is their own breath
and now I am finally learning to love
the sicko I used to try to evict from my head.

A great personality test:
have your subject watch a simulation of an adult
crawling around on all fours
as you quantify their reaction.

A heart beats for x years or so and then it stops.

I Didn't Mean It

There's a space between your words
an ellipsis
hiccups in conversation
where I expect an apology.
These violent impulses in my arms, my hands
this dull rage clawing itself out of my throat
to perch at the center of the table
and stare at us in silence.
Exasperated, I'm losing sight of the point
because there was never one at all
only a feverish mirage.
Genital mutilation, lobotomy almost seem preferable
to this deadly involuntary response
this dangerous reflex.

If it was said unconvincingly, was it really said at all?

Surviving

When he impales you
when he splits you down the middle
you will cry out in pain
claw at his taut skin.
You won't be able to fight him off
but the rape will not break you.
You will mend
even though there will be days when it seems you never could.
You will realize
even though he violated you in the most degrading of ways
he can never strip you of the infinities you possess.
And one day, everything will come flooding back:
not the agony of traumatic memories
but the incandescent strength that has been there all along
the confidence in your recovery.

Prey Drive

Do it, then leave it alone
(at least for a little while).
It festers, that which you've created
an oozing pustule
on someone else's skin.
Some urges are more difficult to deny than others.
Yes, you're just an animal, but put on a dress
and try to act a little more evolved
and interested in the affairs of others.
Pretend you got some scintilla of sleep last night,
that you weren't at the front steps to his apartment
howling that you were going to kill him
until you absolutely had to commute to work.
His neighbors will see the scratch marks on his door
and his bros will see the scratch marks on his back
when he takes off his shirt in the locker room of the gym
to flex for his Snapchat hoes;
he doesn't realize that you're the fox
playing with prey
until you bore and hunger for something more satisfying.

Consent Isn't a Bonus, It Is Mandatory

a necessity
more crucial than that toothpick dangling
lazily between his teeth
a summer heat
your body is romanesque
not to be treated like a dutch colonial
your body is not an anteroom
where he can arrive and depart as he pleases
it is a clandestine study under lock and key
walls lined with sacred texts containing your knowledge
reserved for only those worthy of you
you need to want his keen hands fingering
the spines of your volumes
as much as he wants to
or else he doesn't belong in your space
nor does he deserve to browse.

Stria

stretch marks:
the most beautiful thing to grace a woman's body
to bless the fecund earth
they are wild, striking tigers
striping stripped hide
there is nothing like the dimpled flesh
of the soft feminine form
like the skin of a clementine
ready and fresh to be plucked
to be peeled
to be devoured
ready for its juices to dribble from your mouth
and puddle at your feet
bring you to your knees.

Butisntallbeautyreal

not sorry my feet don't smell like lavender
but I bet hers do
I bet they're redolent of powderfreshness
when I work out, I'm drenched with sweat
I don't glimmer with a donutglaze, a slicksheen of sugar
my skin isn't bottlebronze or any hue close to that color
my pallor is a ghostly pinkpale burning scarlet in the summer
and under the gaze of a lover
my face is far from symmetrical
but in fine art it is asymmetry that is considered beautiful.

I am not the sort of plasticbeauty to be exposed
on the cover of a zine
I am not a fuckablebeauty to be loved
only when between the sheets
I am a realbeauty to be appreciated
for all of the flaws of my exterior
and deeper
and deeper.

Don't Tread on Me

snake coiled on your skin
inked emblem of freedom
warns of hostile planes I stretch my spine to cross
of sins that my next molting will shed

I am not perched on your arm
but still slithering and serpentine
you bit into the pomegranate I offered
and swallowed every seed

cold-blooded, I sun myself in the heat of your shame
I bask in your mutinous desire for ugliness
my forked tongue flits and I smell the disgust
that only makes you want me more

you can't touch my scales, but you can look
if you promise not to stare

you can believe my words if you promise not
to hear where they splinter into lisping hisses

if you pretend not to notice how my body is
barely soldered together
as you peel off my snakeskin dress
of last season's mistakes

In the Genes

These demons in my genes
whispering that thebottle/thepills/themadness will get me
like they corroded the rest of my family
if I'm tempted
or if I allow myself to capitulate to snakes.
Yet I resist
fearing slack sallow skin
and a brain that slips out of my ears onto the piss yellow floor.
Diseases of the mind that rot us from the inside out
until we abandon our mansions and sleep in the streets
forget how to clean ourselves after we shit;
mouths stitched shut with dull shared needles
so that we can never gossip about the other sicknesses
and the electric shock treatments.
Toxic, toxic
everything in my heart.
I poisoned the last fool who let me infect him
with my dirty blood;
surely I would poison you, too.

Grieving

Don't remind me what day it is;
this harsh light and these strong smells
are too much for my senses to bear
on this saturnine day.
I don't want to recover;
leave me here to languish in these fermenting sheets.

In my grief
I don't want to heal:
this pain is much more comfortable,
all too familiar.

Exploration XXX

Indecisive,
not sure what you like yet
(but who says you have to make up your mind?)
Tentative,
your teeth hesitating on your bottom lip
(who says you have to decide?)
Wavering,
your form in space:
one moment trembling, and the next
deathly still.
Quivering,
betraying more with your nervous sweat
than your words could ever convey;
don't fear me
or this abrupt closeness.

Sapphic

Human bacteria
we like warm, wet, dark things:
pierced nostrils
hairy armpits
caves
the rancid heat between your legs.
Together we breed in claustrophobic privacy
sex that won't spawn any offspring.

Denial

The field study of anatomy
is nothing to fear, right?
I mean, I have a vagina too—
fuck.
Frozen in space, in time—
wait.
It's a continuum, remember?
I've forgotten everything in this tactile moment.
identity as muddled and fluid as
my feelings for the boy who introduced me to love
with his clenched fist.
This can't be love, it's something else;
I'm still owned, someone else's property.
his name is still engraved here after all these years,
beneath my left clavicle.
Do you like what I like?
Do you feel confused too?
The terror of betrayal makes me quiver
like desire does to you in my presence.
What is this,
what am I,
frankly I have no idea.
Having an existential crisis
as you moan my name
while invading the neutral country that is my mouth
with the small army that is your tongue.

Tabula Rasa

As an artist I bring beauty to blank slates
but there is something about your unsullied canvas
so unbearably captivating
that I can't allow myself to love you.
You are so pure:
so innocent and benign
your soul so virginal
sheltered from the pain of loss, of betrayal
and human depravity.
I am marred by the trauma I have endured
but not broken
not seeking someone to fix me
or make me whole.
I am complete on my own:
by overcoming adversity I have realized my worth.
If I permitted myself to love you
I would engulf you; my colors would stain your tablet.

Some of the most beautiful works of art
are best left untouched
and admired from far away.

Dream-eater

In the basement's loaded darkness, he offered me a
drink. I flinched at its viscosity, its luminescence.
Its thickness was sharp in my mouth, like
Sprite infused with small shining beings.
Breaking above ground, I stumbled into a
dimly lit lot to the new unfurling of
hidden worlds. I couldn't see them before
he made me cry scales.
In the lot, I watched huge slugs huddle
around burning trash. They were lifting
bright orbs from the fire,
they were eating dreams.
Their subterranean slime awakened the
residue coating my tongue. I had to run back,
I forgot something in the basement. But when I descended,
I couldn't remember what my mind had erased.

To the Person I Will Someday Love

you don't have to be all ropy muscle and baritone
sinewy like an ancient oak
being the epitome of masculinity is not a necessity to be with me
hush
I know how the ideals society has impressed upon you
since you were a child
have left you broken
so with me, be as you are
whatever and whoever that may be
((whatever gender identity))
for it is exquisite in its more-than-maleness
own your every emotion
let expression stream from your eyes without shame
without fear
for I am here not to dry your tears
but to help you learn from them
I am here to hear you
to listen
to be all the reassurance you will ever need that you are enough.

Everything You Need Is Already Within You

I can begin if I choose
but I am not ready to.
The start is the part of this story
I fear the most;
I hide from what my life could be,
staying in bed and dreaming
of the alternate universes that may exist
in which I do not doubt myself.
These worlds are invisible
but if I could slice through space and time
to meet the better version of myself
and ask for her advice,
what would she reveal?
Would she whisper the words
I have been waiting to hear all of my life?
Maybe she would only smirk and say,
you've known the answer all along.

Emergence

Trippingly, I stumble toward the light
a drunken moth dizzed
by the sure sunshine.
The darkness is consoling only for a while
until you feel it start to seep into your skull
and you need to resurface.
In the light your scars are illuminated
but each scourge tells a story.
You weave tales lambent enough
to coax sighs from the shadows.

Obsolete

plug in and know all
corroded wires leave me unenlightened
clouded by obsolescence I respire
and my breath beads their screens
how could they see me?
their lives are entangled yet
hinge on observation
no circuit board, my own goes unseen
excess cannot constrain me
the only electricity that galvanizes here
is the saltwater that warms my instant coffee
so I reject the infinite
all real numbers known
but I am left with 35 to infinity
never knowing what it will feel like to have a home
other than scratchy, purple wool blankets
ringing bells and paper books
information universal, they still choose ignorance
manacled to screens while we're shackled by chains
instead, let me be nothing
zero a referent for possibility
mining the mantissa of a failed experiment
I'll log (the numbers between nothing and everything)
and maybe I can find something more real
than artificial intelligence and judges and jurists and stingers

Bildungsroman

Whatever you thought you knew was wrong.
You will not be given an explanation;
that's just the way things end sometimes.

The way things begin:
salt blooms on your petals,
lashes ready on your tongue.
You cannot expect the stars to justify themselves;
they only hang there silently.

And the middle, the middle:
this radioactive half-life
this quaking voice like a dawn that never rises to sing
this moonlit path that will bring you home.

Meted Deathbed

Meted death,
condemned to roam
a subterranean realm
which hope cannot transcend.
No room for growth,
I gnaw my chains, a hungry ghost.
In purgatory suffering reigns,
obligatory servitude unsheathes
gaunt eyes seeing all suffering,
bodies bearing the karmic weight
that takes a thousand lives to balance.
Total darkness and silence in the hell of this sphere:
our mangled bodies glow strangely, like alien moons.
I do not know if we reflect the light
torturers live by up above,
stray particles drifting down to our abyss,
or if we emit our own desperate photons,
but we let it guide us:
hideous creatures adapted to suffering.
We see all that they will not let themselves see
our eyes evolving to shadow when blinded,
lips learning shared language when sewn;
if only they knew
they made us more human
when they disposed of us.

Gratitudes

None of this would be possible without Ally Ang. Ally, I will never be able to adequately thank you for believing in my writing enough to be my unpaid/volunteer(!!!!) literary agent, editor, and above all, my friend. Thank you for believing in me, for uplifting my voice, and for opening up doors that would have remained closed without your help. I am so inexpressibly grateful for you.

Deep gratitude to Josh Savory, Catherine Weiss, and to the entire Game Over Books team. I am so grateful that my work has been embraced by such an intentional, ethical, and visionary press.

Thank you to Jane Wong, Jennifer Hwozdek, and Abby Minor for blessing this book.

Thank you to my family: Dad, Nana, Pops, Aunt Ann, Uncle Mike, Aunt Tonya, and Lori. Your decision to support me after all of the harms I am responsible for has saved my life. Thank you for teaching me what unconditional love means. Jimmy Lee and Melanie Werley: you came into my life during my darkest moments and helped me transform it into something beautiful and meaningful. Thank you for teaching me that family isn't something we're born into, it's something we create.

Thank you to my friends, both those who knew me when I was home and have still chosen to support me in spite of everything, and the ones I've made since I've been inside who have taken chances on me: Milah Allison-Smith, Katrina Goodjoint, Olivia Gregory, Olivia Hugosson, Valerie Kiebala, Lillian Leibovich, Ellen Melchiondo, Emma Schwartz, and Sara Sensemen. I love you all so, so much. Thank you for teaching me the meaning of friendship.

To my legal team at the Juvenile Law Center, Holland & Knight, and The Youth Sentencing and Reentry Project, especially Marsha Levick, Riya Shah, and Annie Ruhnke: thank you for believing in me and for all of your hard work on my behalf. Thank you for genuinely caring about me, for seeing me as a whole person and not just a client. Thank you for teaching me that my life and my freedom are worth fighting for.

Thank you to Luna Fernandez, Enid Santiago, and all of the incredible people at SELF! Reentry Lehigh Valley. You have no idea what a privilege it has been for me to witness how many women you have empowered and how many lives you have changed. Luna and Enid, thank you for being my friends and for supporting me for all of these years. Even though your work centers women returning home from prison, you continue to show up for and support me throughout this long and uncertain fight for freedom. I can't wait to join you when that day finally comes for me!

Thank you to Holy Trinity Memorial Lutheran Church and the Morning Glories for embracing me as a member of the congregation. Thank you for teaching me that community transcends prison walls.

Thank you to GeGe, Adams, and all the other Canine Partners for Life puppies I've had the honor of training, working with, living with, and falling in love with. Thank you for teaching me how to be patient, trustworthy, and responsible. Thank you for reminding me of my humanity. Thank you for enduring my endless hugs, kisses, and torment and reciprocating with slobber.

Finally, I have to thank all of the folx at SCI Muncy I've been doing this time with: thank you for being my community. Thank you for being the ones I turn to when it's all too heavy to carry, for the mutual aid work we do every single day to survive. Thank you for teaching me that we can consciously choose to be the light in such a dark place, that we all have the potential to grow, learn, and change. Our stories matter, and I promise that I will never stop fighting until we're all free.

Biography

Jamie Silvonek (she/her) is a writer, activist, prison abolitionist, and college student at Ohio University. She has written for The Prison Journalism Project, The Juvenile Justice Information Exchange, George Washington University's Women in Beyond the Global, and numerous social justice zines. At 14, Jamie was sentenced to 35 years to life in prison, which she is serving at SCI Muncy in Pennsylvania. In her spare time, she enjoys training dogs, tutoring, working out, reading nerdy books, stuffing her face, and challenging misconceptions about incarcerated human beings. *Marginal Verse* is her first book of poetry.